Waterbound

Poems by April Pameticky

Kansas City   Spartan Press   Missouri

Spartan Press
Kansas City, MO
spartanpresskc@gmail.com

Copyright © April Pameticky 2019
First Edition 1 3 5 7 9 10 8 6 4 2
ISBN: 978-1-950380-53-4
LCCN: 2019947873

Design, edits and layout: Jason Ryberg
Cover image: Jon Lee Grafton
Title page image: Melody Sircoulomb
Author photo: Tye Pameticky
All rights reserved. No part of this publication may be reproduced or transmitted in any form or by any means, electronic or mechanical, including photocopying, recording or by info retrieval system, without prior written permission from the author.

Acknowledgments:

The author would like to thank the editors of the following publications where some of these poems originally appeared:

"Hair" & "Goldfish," *Gasconade Review,* Fall 2018
"The Fracture" & "Pregnant" *Chiron Review,* #101 September 2015
"Nineteen" *Chiron Review,* Summer 2011
"You do not Write Poems about Rhinoceri, but You wish You Did" *Sand River and Other Places I've Been,* Finishing Line Press 2013
"What Happened After the Lock-Down Drill" *Turtle Island Quarterly,* Spring 2019
"In Middle School" *Malpais Review,* Summer 2015
"Bug-Eating" *The Shocker,* WSU Alumni Magazine, Spring 2014
"Road Church," *River City Poetry,* chapbook
"Anatomy of a Sea Star," Casa de Cinco Hermanas Press, Summer 2015, chapbook
"Skipping Stones" *Mikrokosmos,* June 2011

TABLE OF CONTENTS

Chapter 1 / **Kneeling**

Hair / 1
Smoke Rings of Sound / 3
Mysterium ad Infinitum / 4
We Don't Speak of It / 5
The Fracture / 7
Nineteen / 9
The Grasses Speak / 12
Give Me Your Mourning / 13
You Do Not Write Poems About Rhinoceri,
   But You Wish You Did / 14
Grief Comes Calling for Afternoon Tea / 17
This I Believe / 18

Chapter 2 / **Teacher**

Teacher / 21
Public Humiliation Part 1 / 23
What Happened After the Lock-Down Drill / 24
In Middle School / 27
Public Humiliation Part 2 / 28
Ten O'Clock News / 29
Paper / 30
Student Portrait 1: Hunger / 31
Student Portrait 2: Mute / 33
Student Portrait 3: Trigger Warning / 35
Public Humiliation Part 3 / 36

Chapter 3 / **The B Sides**

Scrape Part 1 / 38

Bug-Eating / 39

Cracked / 40

Binge / 41

Moth / 42

Meta / 43

Scrape Part 2 / 44

Thelonious Monk / 45

Big Bird / 46

Mirrors / 47

Shoulders / 48

Swallow / 49

The Trouble with Poetry / 50

True Story / 52

Bus Stop on a Thursday / 54

Scrape Part 3 / 55

Kale / 57

Coincidence / 58

Road Church—

   July 2016 / 59

   Fall 2014 / 60

   Summer 1994 / 61

   Christmas Eve 2003 / 62

   Now and Then / 64

Chapter 4 / **Waterbound**

Goldfish / 67

The Body, Liquid / 69

Anatomy of a Sea Star / 70

Pregnant / 78

A Thousand Gallons of Water / 80

Catfish / 81

Eyes Closed / 83

Before Dinner / 84

Skipping Stones / 85

Fishes and Loaves / 86

Rain / 90

For Tye, Leia, & Mara Jade

*In one drop of water are found all the secrets
of all the oceans...*

—Kahlil Gibran

Chapter 1
Kneeling

Hair

I collect my hairs from shower drains,
caught on brass door handles, scraped off
wall pockmarks, car ceilings, desk drawers,
the shadow whiskers on his face,
corners where tile meets drywall,
endless maws of the vacuum, swirls and mats.

Victorian families collected hair of their dead,
twisting strands onto tangled snarls of curling wire,
blooming flowers, growing wreaths
showing so many shades of keratin brown.
Displays would expand as households would shrink,
heirlooms passed from mother to daughter,
aunt to heir, memento mori.

Proper ladies made brooches, corsages,
writing letters on their techniques.
Pam and I found a hair museum on a road trip
to Independence. Lost and curious,
we twisted our own hair around twitching fingers,
considered the inhuman colors
modern dyes allowed modern us,.

My children, a genetic lottery,
wheat waves, and amber corkscrews,
mixed from the same parental soup,
flags shining in the afternoon sun.

Dee insisted that I cut their curls,
just a few, she hid them away
in a safety deposit box among
her opals and jeweled rings,
sealed in plastic bags, air pressed out,
where she kept curls of her own children.

My husband leaves the white sink powdered
in fine, dark hairs after a shave,
reminder that I need to clean out the snarls trapped
in our glass shower.
I drag my index finger,
spelling out *Hair* like a child would finger
Wash Me on the back
of a dirt-encrusted Chevy in a Wal-Mart parking lot.

Some day I will wish
I had gathered that dust into bags,
kept it near me in wax and twine,
made a brooch of him,
a final clasp.

Smoke Rings of Sound

Music curls around our noses,
cigarette smoke rings of sound.

The pace jigs our knees,
our toes incessantly in motion,
bent at the joint.

We want the noise to bleed
out our thoughts,
the song to take us away from
the wrinkle forming between our brows,

our shared temple of misery
and sand rivers of grief,

the particles of grit and b minors
friction away at bliss.

You laugh, a burst of shattered
mourning,
your eyes too tired for tears,
and you ask me to turn it up,
the player spinning round our hearts.

Mysterium ad Infinitum

Wait,
breathing in stillness,
eyes desperately drawn
to the candlelight and the alter,
back stiffening against
oak pew and futility.

Wait,
breathing in the incense,
the collected hope,
eyes slitted in the attempt
to catch a glimpse of the holy,
knees screaming against
the cold of the kneeler.

Wait,
breathing in the waiting,
the chorus and the ritual,
eyes closed
in exhaustion.

A tug
on arm.
looking down
into that sweetly upturned face,
the two-year old
blue gaze so sure.

Found it,
that something worth waiting for,
that intangible essence.

We Don't Speak of It

1.
The quiet gaps between breath and sense,
pretend her stories are truth,
nod though our hearts clench.
She is so scared.
Better to be afraid of the elaborate fabrication
than to realize it's all smoke,
that gremlins move the dust-collecting detritus,
the memorabilia,
her mind crumbling like dry cheese,
meaningless bits and pieces holding her gaps together,
it's all so important
      —if she can just remember why.
We nod in sympathy,
try to put everything back in its exact hollow
so there's never a shadowy ring,
smooth our features to bland depths,
hold her quiet hand as she explains.

2.
Metastatic brain tumors as a result of adenocarcinoma
We look at each other like he's cast a spell,
the doctor in his wrinkled white coat,
because the words mean nothing
      —teeth grinding down like crunched peppermints
      in my worst recurring dreams nothing,
      just mush in my mouth nothing

but it can't be good because good things have simple names
        —roller skating, _____, butterscotch
We learn that cancer eats holes into her brain.
I imagine those tumors like hungry, hungry caterpillars
leaving lace patterns on greenery.

3.
Summer 2000
We've snuck around the corner of the Henning's cheese factory
on our way from Madison,
the texture of warm curd lingering in my mouth
until the smoke inhalation dries my tongue.

She has offered me one of her Virginia Slims,
and I am delighted that we are keeping each other's secret
        —that my husband doesn't know she does,
        and her husband doesn't know I do.

And it's silly to think we were fooling anybody because we reek
when we get back to the car,
despite the powerful peppermint drops we use,
despite that we never smoke in front of them and
the wind is always blowing.

The Fracture

1.
Handfuls of legos and plastic bits all down the hallway,
sharp jagged *momento mori* of smashed castles and
dragons.

She sleeps, one tender arm flung over the edge
of her princess daybed, hair flung over face and moving
with each shallow breath.

You lean against the wall, held up by sleep-exhausted knees
and a basket of laundry, just watch, tandem inhalation.

2.
Your lipstick smears across the outside of your lip-line,
car motion recentering gravity left of your sitbone,

You wish he wouldn't take the turns so fast,
watch the car seat tilt precariously while she claps and
giggles,

Words trapped behind teeth, their currency void in this
market anyway,
wiping skin free of *Gentle Rose* pigment.

3.
The warmth of the pew is lost as you stand, pious eyes
 yielding,
hands flickering through the cross, muscle-memory of
 salvation.

He crowds you, his shoulder bumping yours,
snapping to quiet her high-pitched curiosity,

Do this in remembrance of me, the bowing a shared
motion at the Fracture,
and you know that you can't let him keep driving the car.

Nineteen

In the summer of 2010, my daughter turned two,
the heat blanket-thick, too hot to sleep, too moist to be awake,
wet behind the knees and in all the private creases.
Walking through the door, I stripped down to bra and panties,
baby down to diaper, and we ran
like blonde Cherokee through the house.

On the morning Leah passed,
a gray pigeon slammed into my classroom window,
the glass hip-high to ceiling, a twelve-foot expanse
of sunshine and crackling spiderwebs on impact.
The bird's neck cracked a final bend as I tried
to pull eager students back from the view.
They did not know death when they saw it.

Disjointed with pale efforts and a drought of words—
A kind word uttered and repeated... a star
fallen from the blue tent upon the green carpet.*

I was nineteen when I met her
in the crisp fall of '96—
fresh soil and she was wisdom and water,
and her smile glittered so brightly I would just bask.
I want to be fluid for her,
give forth lines that make meaning of
helpless and *cancer.*

The darkness comes,
that place I dwell with nothing
left to pour forth—
*In the depth of my soul there is a wordless song ... it refuses
to melt with ink on parchment.**
My ink is the cracked residue,
the pigeon-cracked window.

She handed me The Prophet. *This is for you.*
and I said,
Speak to me of friendship,
And she answered, *Let there be laughter.**

Down a white gravel lane, I once rode in a carriage
restored and preserved, her father silent beside me
as he drove some wide-open stranger his
daughter brought home like an eager stray.
How many of us had he seen?
I cascade with words and rain and
too many such moments
for coherence.
I remember that while I twisted
and struggled to be,
knotted around in my darkness,
she stood firm in the light,
no fear of the day,
and she just knew herself,
Solid.

Perhaps she was saying, even as that gray bird
stepped off his branch into flight,—

*Let me sleep, for my soul is intoxicated with love,
and let me rest, for my spirit has had its bounty
of days and nights.**

I want to do right, frame her radiance so others will know
But I mourn, grieve rivers that flow from the center
and I watch pieces of me float away.

Then I remember fall twilight and crisp air.
I imagine she picks me up from the bookstore
in her ketchup red '62 Volkswagon.
I am nineteen and she plays mix tapes
of Leonard Cohen and the Beastie Boys
all the way out to Ponca lake
with our bottle of strawberry Boone's Farm.
We sit on a musty car blanket and tell
stories under the stars.

* from Kahlil Gibran's *Tears and Laughter*

The Grasses Speak

The smell of lush soil and verdant moss
surrounds, like a toddler,
I want to dig through the gravel for some small treasure,

some shell to keep in my pocket,
to remind me of time-swept oceans on our dry plain,
a memento to remind me of what this space feels like,

right here overlapped by right now,
the sun warming the soreness from my gut and shoulders.
I know there will never be enough breakfast to feed this day.

Grasses grow from a pot, flowing, blowing
tendrils of hair, the tips furry and splayed in the wind.
I want to dwell among them,

listen to the sweet tenor of the Soil Sisters
putting their fingers to dirt,
sending prayers through the ground,

sweet thoughts travelling up roots,
lifted more pure to heaven.
They whisper, *Speak to me of eternity,*

and the grasses sing,
You have been there,
but you have forgotten the memory.

We grasp soil, our fingers desperate and praying to know.

Give Me Your Mourning

Give me your mourning,
the tired tears
when the eyes are brittle dry;

The walk into empty rooms,
the stunned moment of *Why did I come in here?*

The smells of slowly rotting food
left too long in the kitchen trash.

Give me the ache resting in the finger joints,
the pang of wrist holding hand holding head.

Give me his side of the closet,
his shoes holding a little next of spiders,
the cobwebs in corners only he could reach.

There's a pile of envelopes with his name,
give me that, too.

Give me your effort to stand after sitting too long in his chair.

You Do Not Write Poems About Rhinoceri, but You Wish You Did

1.
You sit in the back, the chair functionally
uncomfortable, and wonder what you are doing
in the basement atrium
—you were never her student,
never allowed yourself to be a poet.
Concealed carefully under your coat
is the chapbook you purchased here.
You pretended you already owned it,
had always been a follower,
were familiar with her work.
You sit in the back and marvel.

2.
A debate rages for the family *rhinocerotidae*
as to the plural form of that
giant, horn-bearing herbivore.
You are warned not to fall into
the rhinoceri trap,
to beware of making this egregious,
pompous error,
although you still believe that
rhinoceroses is a little like
fishes and *mooses*.

You want to own rhinoceros
like you own grief,
that river that you *know*,
but curiosity requires energy
imagination
you don't always get enough fiber.

3.
You took a class because you still secretly
believe one can *learn* to write.
They were so excited,
so pleased to be a part of the struggle,
and they shared around,
admiring and snapping fingers in metrical homages to effort.
In their sweetheart-butterscotch way,
they only wanted to give you permission,
the *nod* to take what you already owned.
The irony of all the degrees, notebooks,
rejections piled in the corner with dust
and clots of cat fur
all announcing I am a Writer
has not escaped you.

4.
You sit on the couch,
the one that smells like feet and dog.
It used to be fashionably Taupe,
now more the color of grit
collected under your nail.

You sit on the couch
with your phone in your hand.
You must make meaning from what you have learned,
and you struggle to find words for the soundless dark.
Grief is beside you eating cereal
straight from the box,
his arm a slow weight across your shoulders
as your head fills with sand.

5.
Poems about rhinoceri are never
really about rhinoceri.

Grief Comes Calling for Afternoon Tea

I have gouged
out a few handfuls

of inches from my torso
so that I may serve

jam and scones at tea,
folded in my shallow

breaths for a hint
of sweetness and cream,

vacuumed the rug,
dusted under the coffee table—
      for grief always judges the housekeeping,

made myself presentable
in mauve and rose,
plucked my eyelashes for garnish.

This I Believe

I believe in the *Sacrum Vis*,
the force,
the fascia web that binds all of our innards from
becoming our outards,
the holy energy that sparks
where poems flow forth,
that moment where God breathed on Adam and We
became Word.

I believe a river flows forth,
*Big Magic,**
our bodies the cup,
sacred vessel, marauding pirate ship.
We can float free and never touch,
or we can tap in, all in, and become Word.

I believe when we are hurt,
and we are always in some way hurt,
we tuck in, roll, bury,
grow scar tissue, harden.
And we can't always drink
or even know that water is there.

I believe in the journey,
the seeking,
the deliberate
on purpose
put your keys in the car and your bag in the trunk
Come ON, we're GOING trip.

To seek for the well is to drink from the Word.

I believe this is not always an easy trek,
that to be silent and listen feels like a scratchy pair of socks,
that there's no GPS tracker,
or perfect route,
only rocks on the path and an empty canteen
and a belief that water is just up the way.

I believe that what we have must be shared.
Like fishes and loaves,
there will be more.
Just not always when we want it or expect it.
But we keep to the road,
and sing travelling songs.

I believe in the *Sacrum Vis,*
that onus weighing on an artist's soul
to stretch and push
and create.
That place Where poems flow forth,
and We become both Adam and the Wind.

I believe a river flows out
and in for all of us,
our bodies merely the cup
the vessel.
We can float free and never touch,
or we can tap in, all in, and become Word.

*With special thanks to *Big Magic* author Elizabeth Gilbert and Julia Cameron's *The Artist's Way*

Chapter 2
Teacher

Teacher

Today I am foot sore and sweat.

I am box full of sharpened #2s,
    buzzword and bully.

I am all heart and no room left for gains,
    balloon,
    and chalkdust
    and expo smeared on cheek.

I am *Dream Deferred,*
    hungry faces
    and all our best efforts.

Today I am part TedTalk,
    part cawing crow
    and *Tyger Burning Bright.*

I am cadence and support,
    masking tape, glue-gun,
    real gun
    and fear.

I am *rage against the dying of a light.*

I am dinner served from a box,
    too tired and well-spent.

I am high-five and fist bump,
        scold and side-hug.

I am broken puzzle box and tear-saturated tee,
        spare coins for snack
        and mandatory reporter.

I am *the powerful play*
        and I might contribute a verse.

Today I am love and hope and sorrow
        to return day after day.
        Teacher.

---

*Dream Deferred, Langston Hughes
*The Tyger, William Blake
*Do Not Go Gentle Into That Good Night, Dylan Thomas
*Oh Me! Oh Life! Walt Whitman

Public Humiliation Part 1

You watch as she explains to him
it's not you, it's me
I just don't want to ruin our friendship
You applaud her poise in telling him that
But you see the way his happiness melts off his face
and he slumps 2 inches shorter.

You want to interrupt,
tell him that there will be others,
there will be wonderful and awful others,

but you are pretending that they can't see you,
the supervising adult in the hallways.

They are pretending they can't see you
while everyone is a backpack river flowing around them,
everyone is watching,
ignoring the worst day of his life.

What Happened After the Lock-Down Drill

We are settling back into our desks when
He asks me *What would you do?*
My keys still stuck in the door,
the question they all want to know
        and maybe they've asked other teachers,
           or maybe now just seemed like the right time,
but he asks *What would you do, Miss?*
and even the talkers in the back grow silent to listen.

I look at his sweet face, his earnest eyes,
at the girl behind him,
the one that can't stop brushing her hair in class,
at the boy to her left, so meticulous
about his clothes and his punctuation,
at all of them in various shades of growing up,

I look at them and wish I could tell them I was going to be a hero,
would stand in front of them
and save them from bullets and crazy classmates,
that I would have the courage to be their shields,
that I wouldn't cower or bow down
but resist
and fight.

Except that's not what I signed up for.
I applied for sharpened pencils and pronoun/antecedent agreement,
a smile of triumph at figuring out a difficult analogy,

to empower students with the greatest equalizer of all: words.
I didn't sign up to die,
a soft-target of a self-indulgent reality-star wannabe,
and maybe I'm not capable of standing firm.

Maybe I would curl up in my closet and shiver and pray
that the shooter would get them first
before ever seeing me
so that I could go home to my own kids
and all of these locusts are on fire in my brain
when I'm looking at my students
all staring at me
and expecting that I love them
so I can't tell them of the bad dreams where I see one of them
with a gun,
of the secret plan to raise the window and escape
out the third-story window by the roof-access ladder,
of the golf club I keep so I can break windows and arms,
of the prayer I say every day when I'm not even sure I believe,

So I tell him,
I will do everything to protect you,
and it's not even a lie right then,
and they are listening and some have soft smiles
because this can never happen to them, they think.

Because that's what teachers do:
memorize the multiplication table
and die in the line of duty.
Second only to soldiers in our bravery,
we knew what we were signing up for,

might even get my name on the
Memorial for Fallen Educators,
next to Catherine Tucker,
Victoria Leigh Soto,
Ed Thomas…
Aaron Feis.
Because there's always room for names.

In Middle School

In middle school,
you learn to sit down and shut up.
You learn to cross your arms and your legs.

You learn it's better, more attractive,
to smile with only a hint of teeth,
to shy away from the snapping bra strap,
to giggle helplessly, cover your mouth coyly,
when you really want
to smack, beat down, breath fire.

In middle school,
you learn to hide your tampons in your sock
nestled near your ankle,
in the waistband of your pocketless pants,
because leggings have no secrets.

You learn to outline your eyes,
blush your cheeks and ripen your mouth,
but keep that tongue
silent
because no one likes
a know-it-all.

In middle school,
you learn to be better with words than numbers,
to pretend you don't understand,
because you're pretty and
that's a more tradable commodity
than all the right answers on all the wrong tests.

Public Humiliation Part 2

It surprised no one when he asked
Her best friend to prom during passing period
after 2nd hour

as he'd been texting and snapchatting
her up all weekend.

He went so far as to make a posterboard sign
Will you kick it w/ me @ Prom
balloons and glitter and awkward shuffles
as he waited for her outside your classroom door
with a row of soccer teammates backing him.

You could never tell if he knew the Old Girl
walked his New Girl
to class everyday,

but it was clear by the nuclear holocaust on Her face
that she wasn't expecting to be supplanted so quickly,

at least New Girl said *yes*,
smiling and red.

Ten O'Clock News

Charlie-dog curled up in my lap, allowed despite dirty feet smell, her warmth seeping down tired legs, fur matted in fists as we watch the news together.

The anchorwoman does that strange smile-speak of journalists, her brow a study in concern, her incongruous mouth turned up,

She is the rector of my nightly ritual, her polish a high shine, her harmonious voice.

A man walked into a school, familiar plaster and cinder block walls,
walked in with his assault rifle, shot

terrified kindergartners as they huddled in cabinets, pushed aside construction paper, glitter glue, stickers.

Tiny bodies shivered as they sang in their heads
I'm a Little Teapot.

Paper

or the day we made paper pinwheels
instead of shooting each other

We folded carefully along
perforated lines, to bend paper

into submission
only to be blown about
by Wichita Wind.

Prescribed in chaotic rolls,
it's so easy in our pale protection

and privilege and innocence
to play at peace
with paper gestures

while Syrian refugees
cross the Mediterranean to be

cast out on the coast,
tiny babies wrapped
in their father's turbans, blue

from cold and starving.

Student Portrait 1: Hunger

Right now he's got his head bowed,
his dark eyes trained on the paper in front of him,
his knee bouncing in time
to the heating unit blower
tap-tap-tapping.

But just before
he will tell you how his mom's
been gone for the last three days,
it's just been him and his sis;
she don't cook real good and
he's *tired of tuna and crackers* and
don't you think his sister should learn to cook
something better?

You will not correct his grammar
or pass judgment
on sibling culinary effort.
You'll just be relieved he at least has
something to eat
because last week he cleaned out
your stash of granola bars and snack packs
you keep hidden in the back file cabinet.
You haven't had a chance to buy more

because you spent that little extra at the bookstore,
buying that book you thought he might actually try to read,
a Kwame Alexander in verse with
the kind of rhythm and language he would appreciate.

Right now he's got his head bowed
but his pencil is in his hand
and you know the assignment is giving him a headache,
but he's trying,
hasn't argued about any of it,
thanked you when you handed him that pencil.

Student Portrait 2: Mute

She has never spoken aloud
to a single classmate in your fourth hour class,
although by January you have now spent nearly
twenty consecutive weeks together,
minus a holiday break where you were concerned
she wouldn't return to school
because she's on a special transfer,
and her parents are tired of you calling home.

Occasionally she's absent
and you ask her peers if they've seen her
and they invariably ask *Who?*

She waits after the bell,
phantasm of patience,
until every rowdy and boisterous teenager
has left the room.
She can safely navigate the desks
and your podium without fear of jostling.
You have watched this ritual all year long.

You've called the social worker,
the ESOL building specialist,
her administrator,
her brother who acts as translator,
her other teachers.

You've used word
after word
after word

but while others have seen what you've seen,
the parents keep asking
Is she in trouble?
Is she misbehaving?
Does she do her work?
We don't understand.
What's the problem?

that it's normal for a fifteen-year-old girl to be silent,
a ghost that no one sees but you,
      —And sometimes she is right in front of you before
you even see,
that she doesn't flirt
or laugh at off-color jokes,
or even make eye-contact for more than a split-second,

and when she does,
you see deep deep into a lake of dread,
don't see me don't see me.

You accidently made her cry that time
by asking too many questions
in front of her classmates,
and she was shaking and trembling
and you just wanted to hug her.

Even now you are clenched scared
that she's just going to disappear,
fade away, and no one will notice she's gone.

Student Portrait 3: Trigger Warning

She is tense,
hands gripped rubber-band tight,
weighing each word in hushed quiet.

She tells you she thinks there should've been a trigger warning
before everyone read that part of the book, the part with
the friend of the father that touches the daughter with his hands,
touches her in a way no girl that age should be touched,
*you know, Miss, because some people might need a warning
before they read stuff like that,*
and she's talking to you secretly,
back by your desk with some sweet illusion of privacy,
because that kind of graphic stuff can be painful,

and you know,
in that sickening place where your stomach used to be,
what she's really telling you
and you want to hug her and say #me too,

but that crosses lines you're not supposed to cross,
so instead you say,
You are probably right.
When we discuss this in class,
I'll handle it very delicately,
and she smiles at you,
relieved that you agree,

and maybe she even knows that you know now
because she's smart like that
and sometimes you just want to burn the world down.

Public Humiliation Part 3

You do not want to see anymore,
do not want to know that kids their age
get up to things like that,

although you vaguely remember what it was like
to wrestle tongues in the hallway,
to pretend the door provided enough cover,

as everyone pretended to not see what you were doing,
the smell of his exhalation,
the feel of his short hair at the nape of his neck.

You don't want to remember all that as you watch him
walk New Girl to class every day,
don't want to remember that the former you
still resides in the current you,
so you turn around and walk quickly to your desk,
shuffle pencils around,
pretend you never went to Prom.

Chapter 3
The B Sides

Scrape Part 1

Scraping fingerpads along concrete pilings,
skin snags on rusted rebar,
watches blood swell slowly,
inflated balloon at the tip,
fairy dew drop,
balance keeps from leaving self behind,
walks heel to toe like a tightropewalker,
gives in,
finally,
tags out initials,
Smears.

Bug-eating

I dared you
to eat a cockroach
because we'd finished *How to Eat Fried Worms*.
Somehow
that all made sense,
that you would eat
that bug
and become super cool,
crunching the exoskeleton
like kettle-cooked chips. But you couldn't bring it
to your mouth
and a thousand days later,
I can't really blame you.
But I wonder if maybe we shouldn't have done it,
all those summers ago,
just to say
we had.

Cracked

Today I am the missing reading glasses,
the late arrival to the staff meeting,
the E on the gas tank,
the left behind lunch.

Tomorrow I will give a friend a ride,
will have all the right-sized envelopes and stamps,
and will manage to have erasable blue or black ink
that never needs white-out.

But today I must push through all the rocks
brought on by hubris,
the sweater stains,
the spilt coffee from the cracked mug.

Binge

There was that time he swallowed
your entire brain, tongue, clavicle, spleen,
navel, knee, phalanx metatarsal,

all the space between good morning coffee
and turning the ignition key, voracious appetite,
eating the tiny details of day,

inhaling the college-rule paper, ticonderoga #2 pencils,
the special gel pens with unsmearable ink,
the grit in the curve of ear cartilage and cuticle,

and still more, he wanted all the exhalations, the cigarette breath,
the forward thinking and aft, swirling inattention and the
focal point of retina, the curve of smile, the empty gesture.

Moth

I am sorry for the moth
trapped
between the screen and tempered glass,

the small muttering movements
slowing to stillness.

I could raise the sash,
let him inside to a semblance of freedom
made more temporary
by all the other closed doors and windows.

But I don't,
watch him gasp back and forth.

I am no tight-fisted child
to be forgiven for careless curiosity.
I decay with every lack of action,
a conscious choice to let that piece fall way
even as the moth drifts softly to the tracks between.

Meta

You discover that metamorphosis
means the full gelatinous mutiny of the caterpillar,
that he must devolve down to a muddle of cells and matter,

no similar frame simply growing wings,
but a full destruction of being,
a puddle.

You wonder if he remembers the taste of milkweed
as he pushes free from his chrysalis,
knows the ground by his belly,

or if he awakens to dismiss it all
as the nightmare
of a mad butterfly.

Scrape Part 2

She has dragged her bike home a full two blocks,
the bmx kuwahara dad built just for her height,
rescued frame from a junk pile,

Rad Racing sticker slapped on crossbar,
Only now handle-bars reversed,
the left pedal turned perpendicular,

you did not hear her coming,
your normal mom radar strangely silent
as you sit at the dining room table,
sipping coffee and playing tetris on your phone,

She is torn, her clothes bloody,
the palm of her hand a cherry rash,
her knee an homage to fresh asphalt and oil slick.

She grins in your face as you see her mess,
but she has managed to drag her own bike home,
has refused to cry the tears held hostage,

her lip jagged and her nose purple.
Shoulda' worn the knee pads, huh she says.
You refuse the urge to cuddle her close,

to coo over every blood badge.
You take your own deep breath
because she's not reaching out to you,

not bawling as she would've only just a year ago.
You see her adultface behind the babyfat,
the grit.

Thelonious Monk

"Blue Monk" plays smooth in the background.
I sit under the tattered awning of the Cherry Street
Coffeehouse,
    ignoring you fiercely,
        curling into the brick corner,
            my refuge,
while you argue over
whether it's the hard 'T' or softer 'TH,'
casting shade on my ignorance,
a whirlpool of bluster and sharks.

I am emerald rain in the sunshine of a setting sun,
    a storm warning,
        shadows cast along the street.

I won't be letting you walk me home.

Big Bird

As foreign to this prairie as a penguin,
she watches the bloom ready to take flight.

We breed a more modest kind hereabouts, he says,
a thin yellow straw slowing his words to a long drawl.

A study in leather and taupe, his soft cowboy heart offended
by the bright petals cupped gently in his hand
      the colors sharp across the span.

All the stars are a-bloom with flowers* she says,
pinching her lips after, trapping her waterfall of words.

But he knows the bird of paradise,
yellow as the California coast,

will steal her away from the tall grass.
Though she is the daughter of his son,

connected by the farmhouse of his mother,
they are as different as twilight and noon.

*excerpt from *The Little Prince,* Antoine de Saint-Exupery

Mirrors

Scent clings to inner arms
while leaning over the sink,

the curve of the linoleum
countertop in lemonfoil green

digs into hip bones,
pressing across the ceasarean scar.

The toothpaste has grit rubbing away
at food particles trapped between teeth.

His toothbrush is softer than yours.
You watch rivulets of sudsy waste

race toward the chipped edge of the drain.

Don't look in the mirror,
don't face the strange collection of black mascara
clumped in the last corner,
don't look at the hollow darkness beneath your eyes.

Shoulders

Tactile memory,
familiar heat of his shoulder against your own,
the pressure of all the days standing

between then and now,
overcooked eggs and pancakes,
towels folded in halves instead of thirds,

a vacuum that would never learn to run itself,
strung along like hand-blown glass beads
and you holding the broken clasp

before all the pieces can spill and shatter on the floor.
The skin of your shoulder cools under the weight
of ghosts and time.

Swallow

You have allowed the bedcovers
to swallow you,
to hold you in a nest of sheets

and the duvet that smells
of fabric softener and burnt hair,
have hidden your face from the

sliver of sunlight that pierces
between the slats of the Ikea blinds.
Sound muffled by pillow,

air moist and close and hot,
and for nothing and no one
will you allow your own escape.

The Trouble with Poetry*

1.
The trouble with poetry
Is that you try too hard.
You're always trying too hard.

Write less. Breathe more.

2.
I don't know how to feel
about battery-operated candles:
       No flame. Only light.
We're certainly safer from burns.

3.
She has eaten all the cashews
from the can of mixed nuts.

And that's the trouble with poetry
      —too many peanuts and not enough of the good stuff:
      hazelnuts, walnuts,
      brazil nuts.

4.
My heels are cracked earth,
scratching the sheets in the middle of the night

5.
You should have to go to the trouble of striking the match,
watching the flame burst, hold inhalation,
hold light to wick, don't startle or wink,
Alchemy.

Although technically a battery is chemistry
And light is light is light is light is light.

6.
We watch a great horned owl land on the peak
of the neighbor's roof at twilight.
She brings me a lone rock,
        concern etched across her brow in a way
                some future version of herself will debate botox,
concern that the rock is alone and has no other rock friends.

I think we are all rocks.

7.
He has made for me a sanctuary of the back deck,
a fairweather spy hole where I pretend to be embedded at Walden,
only a carriage ride away from lunch with friends.

8.
The trouble with poetry is
what's left unsaid.
We are not all matches.

There's never enough light.

We forget how to hold on
to our pens in the dark.

*in response to *The Trouble with Poetry*, Billy Collins, 2006.

True Story

Remember that time
you took a shit on the restaurant bathroom floor?

Leaving it for the new dish guy you were training,
the one you were supposed to mentor through his broken English.

Do you remember how you told me it was part of his job
       to clean the bathrooms,
           that you even showed him how to add the capful
              of ammonia-rich cleanser in water to mop the floor.

How we hired him so he could send money back to his family,
           hired him instead of your best friend
               that wanted to sell dime bags next to the dish machine.

Do you remember his face when he realized
what was in the corner of men's restroom,

the way he swallowed and closed his eyes to breath
slowly through his open mouth to avoid the smell

You secretly snickered at him,
           he would never know that you left him a gift.

I heard he bought the restaurant a few years ago,
that his wife changed the menu and runs his kitchen
while his boys run the dish room.

I heard you had to reapply for your job,
        down on your luck,
presuming on that old relationship
to pull you from your hole,
the financial mess you made,
needing honest work.
You're sober now, working on step 4.

I heard he smiled big at you,
        welcomed you with open arms,
          hugged you as a friend.

I also heard that on your first day back,
he gave you a roll of small doggie bags
        and some rubber dish gloves, just in case
        the bathroom needed cleaning.

Bus Stop on a Thursday

I wait,
wait for them to get off the bus,
the bus that is full of sound and fury,
fury only small children can feel
because they're small but their fury
is so mighty.

I wait for them,
wait for them to get off the bus,
grateful for buffers
Of distance and glass,
glass that separates me from all the chaos
of forty small bodies
screams
laughter
snarling
all at once,
Chaos.

I wait for them,
wait for them to get off the bus.
There will be few days like these,
days where they're excited to see me,
excited and smiling,
mirrored and shining.
They take my hands,
and we walk home.

Scrape Part 3

When you were a girl,
you got 22 stitches just above your knee,
slamming your thigh into rebar sticking out from cement wall
in a construction zone
you had no business playing in,
the flesh parting like a chicken breast,
hardly any blood,
but a fatty gaping smile that had you going into shock,
your fingertips numb.

Even now, no matter how many bends or twists or runs,
the right knee has a little pocket of skin,
a four inch scar parallel to the floor,
fragile and soft and immune to sun.
You can pinch the skin, jiggle it around,
tell war stories about that time you got cut while in the trenches.

Just make shit up,
because the made-up story is so much better than the real one,
where you had snuck off to swim across the street at the hotel
swimming pool, pretending to be a glamorous guest
because you heard one time that Aerosmith had stayed in that
Marriott, and you weren't supposed to go there but you did,
and you wanted to go back because your girlfriends were still
over there and you knew the front desk people were bored
and would overlook you walking in and out of the lobby
in your swimsuit with beach towel,

but you had to check and see if your mom
was home from work yet,
so you peeked through the downstairs apartment,
cupping your hands around your eyes to cut the glare
    off the sliding glass window.

When you looked in, you saw her, and you darted off,
    in a hurry,
hoping she wouldn't spot you and you could pretend you lost
    track of time
and didn't know she was home yet,

but you were running,
not watching,
tripping your way through the construction zone
between your place and the pool when it happened,
you had to grit your teeth,
lost a strap of your flip-flop,
then the whole shoe,
slammed that knee into rebar,
stumbled your way back home.

Kale

He has tried to make you eat the kale
from the bottom back of the fridge,
that place where all things go to die,

the ham casserole with peas,
the salmon jello-mold,
those bills we're afraid to look at.

You have told him that you'd rather eat his athletic sock
after an all day hike,
but he has infected you with a mad desire

for health and immortality
funded by green leafy things
and nonGMO seeded love.

Coincidence

The world is full of perfect synchronicity,
she says,
autonomous serendipity,

that you put GOOD out in the universe
and that great vi sanctorum responds,
gives and nourishes you

with kale and sex and accidental relationship.
You don't want to buy what's she's selling
but you have exact change in your wallet.

You hand over your faith
counted out in dimes,
kiss her on the cheek in farewell.

RoadChurch

July 2016

They finally sleep from the backseat,
my ears full from the pressure
of all that noise trapped
inside the vestibule of this car.

I can love them like this,
precious,
quiet,
sleep-warm
and soft breath.

We leave the radio off,
watch the road and traffic,
not really part of it,
floating,
heat trapped between his palm and mine.

We won't stop,
not for anything,
not a snack or a sunset or a restroom,
this infinite moment of peace,
the road some kind of perfect.

I can talk to God here,
no pressure or ritual,
just a still second with road hum and cicadas.

Fall 2014

I've cracked the window,
let out the music—
        99 Red Balloons—
and let in the smell of moist ground
after the faint sprinkling,
not even enough to switch on wiper blades.

The rhythm of the road vibrating
up through my thighs
in unpredictable hums
and bumps
and burrs
that blend together.

Western Kansas,
nothing but wind and railroad tracks,
turbines and pumpjacks.

We're on our way to Taos,
two women with a playlist
 and some fashion magazines.

We're both going to be bored
to chewing on our nails,
screeching out song lyrics,
eating too much candy.

We'll both be awed by trees
that look like monsters outside of Philmont.

We'll both be so grateful to find
our hotel with clean sheets and a hot tub
somewhere on the property.

Summer 1994

There was a time after
my stepbrother Ryan died,

his head pressed between the steel frame
of his truck door and the red clay dirt
of the culvert on old Hubbard road,

There was a time when every long row of cars
was the line of mourners that stretched

behind the family limousine, headlights on
in the bright afternoon sunshine,

July heat battered away
by dripping car air conditioners,

the silence trapped like a bubble
inside the limo
and nowhere to get a breath.

There was a time when I would count
other funeral processions

just to see if they had more cars than my brother,
because it just seemed to me at seventeen,

a life could only be measured
in the length of the line of cars.

Christmas Eve 2003

More than once
we've found ourselves

stranded

on some long and lonely road,
not metaphorically,
but literally.

Like that time
our thumbs were out

on a dark Christmas Eve,
while I cried and shivered
because I couldn't decide
if it would be better
to be picked up by a sociopath
or freeze to death by the side of HWY 70.

In my frustration at the death of the car,
I had broken off the brittle interior handle

of the '84 Camaro,
        with its dashboard light effects
        and speedometer bar.
        It's a classic, you said.
        Vintage.

So I got used to sitting low to the ground,
tried not to over-gas it,
spin out the tires,
made the best of it because it was cheap
and we were broke.

Secretly it reminded me
of french-rolled jeans
and tee-shirt barrettes.

But right then,
as something choked
  and sputtered
    and died in that car,
as the power steering went out

and you managed to get us
  over to the shoulder,
    iced over and white,
as I realized that we couldn't just sit

in the car and wait for someone to rescue us,
when I broke off that door handle,
a tiny part of my romantic love for you
    broke off,
      and you became a little chipped.

Now and Then

How did we travel before the Garmin?
Before TomTom or GoogleMaps,
before our cellphone GPS,
when we had to stop for bad directions,
pee on the side of the road,
sleep in our car because we had no idea
there was a hotel just ten miles down the road.

We just got in our cars
and expected to get somewhere.

One time I ended up in Missouri
when I was trying to get to
Eureka Springs, Arkansas.

But I was in my '78 Delta 88,
feeling grown-up following my McNally atlas.

My girls will never know the joy of turning
the map the other way around,

of not being sure just when they'll arrive,
of interpreting gutturals and pointings,
begging for the bathroom key
secured with a toilet-seat-lid.

I've driven the stretch of 1-35
between Wichita and Blackwell
hundreds of times.

I've taken the turn south of Perry
onto the Cimarron turnpike to Tulsa
just as many.

Muscle memory,
vague automaticity takes over.
I'm in a zen sort of boredom,
some Judith Krantz book-on-tape playing,
always some stretch of construction
never finished.

I enter the car one person;
exit it another.

Chapter 4
Waterbound

Goldfish

Last week I was Fish In Bowl,
just me and bubbling pirate's chest.
I could see out,
watch television,
people playing Yahtzee.

All voices muffled,
stretched syllables elongated whale song.

I hunger,
wait for pellets to land on surface,
to float and fly gracefully down.

Last night I was Fish
surrounded by green, comforting and warm,
soft curtains that don't scratch what's left of my scales.

Sometimes I am Bird,
fly above the surface of the bowl,
sing through air as noise blares and screams,

hurt my brain and my eyes dry from wind,
and so when I break the tension of the water,
fall deeper into comforting stillness,

I will lie on bottom gravel for a bit,
taste each pebble in fracture ritual,
list and watch bubbles rise.

Today I swim in circles, tilt and sway.
The bottom is up, the top is so far away.
I wade through murky water for release,
for sustenance, for sound.

The Body, Liquid

Movement
overshadows
thought,
the body,
liquid
poured
smoothly
into a
glass
like warm
chocolate.
She smiles,
teeth
glowing,
hands
speaking
along
the length
of his
spine.

Anatomy of a Sea Star
(A Love Song)

On the nature of the ubiquitous sea star: a defense mechanism against predators, these creatures can regenerate limbs. Near the turn of the twentieth century, angry oysterman, fed up at sea stars eating their catch, cut the sea stars in half, tossing the bodies back overboard. Ultimately, the sea star population doubled in less than a decade, decimating the oysters in the process.[1]

Covered in tiny white spines, members of the phylum echinodermata can excrete their stomach out of their mouths, oozing into partially open clams, digesting the interior, and finally returning to their bodies.[2]

[1] From National Ocean Service, NOAA
[2] From National Geographic Online

1.
Two minutes from now he will tell you again about his day.
The words feel familiar, taste like sediment,
but he can't be sure if it was you the first time through,
you that laughed about that mishap during his meeting,
you that mirrored his frown at all his frustrations,
you that he made love to against the hollow office door.
Three minutes from now,
you will nod and release a braying laugh,
the sound spilling like milk between you.
Making excuses and backing away,
you slide into shadow.

2.
The first time he spoke to you,
you can't remember it,
pretend it happened at the Connestoga truck stop off of 1-35,
create whole fictions from scraps of memory.
Maybe you talked poetry,
Bill Clinton,
cheese fries,
Jesus,
the endless burnt coffee,
smoking your way through so many great ideas.
This will not be the last thing you lie over.

3.
You offer a small morsel from your own plate,
the steak meat succulent red,
watch his mouth tighten, close.
His head tilts away
as he explains the he doesn't eat from another's plate,
though he will eat at your flesh later.
You feel he has hacked a limb,
tossed you back
into the sea,
stunted.

4.
In the darkness, you lie in the divot
your body has made in the mattress over time,
listen to his quiet breathing, the rhythmic inhalations,
imagine his body in the quiet dark,
occupying his own shallow trench.
You tense and twitch, sleep a lost cause.

He rolls,
the wave of the bed,
the weight of him,
your hair beneath,
trapped.

5.
The furniture of your lives gathers dust,
hardwood planks glaring between you,
the distance stretched,
yawning,
an exclamation point,
miles of prairie and buffalo scattered wide,
all those confetti moments unspoken,
a barrel of fish swimming frantic unending crop circles.
Thoughts of getting up
    —crossing that distance,
       making room for yourself in that space,
are hidden behind the mask of what's unsaid,
unfelt,
the unknown just too much to carry.

6.
When you hear his voice,
it's from deep beneath,
gargled and bubbled,
the syllables swallowed and softened by saltwater waves,
I love you,
he says,
but it's muffled.

7.
You lie in the grass,
smell lush soil, verdant moss.
You dig fingers in the dirt
for some smidgen of treasure,
some little shell to keep in a pocket,
a freshwater conch memento
of time-swept oceans long gone on this plain,
a token of what this space feels like,
right here
overlapped
by right now,
the sun warming the soreness
from gut and shoulders.
There will never be enough breakfast
to feed this day.

8.
Sand gets in all the creases, grit and filth
beneath your nails,
crusting the pink of your nailbeds,
shadows creasing your torso
and the knees of your jeans.
You will shower together today,
sharing shampoo and space,
his warmth seeping,
his voice resonant and echoing,
strangely clear,
I love this,
he says.
You believe him,
your fingers lost in the thick
darkness of his hair.

9.
Your skin hungers to touch, to feed, but each caress
slides into nothing, adrift.
He will smile at you, showing the curve of his mouth
and dimple, but it's a smile he gives easily
and to everyone,
the same for the cashier,
the brake guy,
your mother,
you—midcoitus.

10.
You pretend a conversation with him that never occurs,
imagine funny quirks that don't exist,
repeat a story as if it happened,
    —and it *did* happen for a moment because you spoke it,
lie in attribution, saying things he never says,
all while too lonely to touch,
your skin extended beyond your sight,
hungry for something that may never be,
the smell of him lost.

11.
He tells you
I am an artist.
You nod your head like you know what that word means
beyond canvas and splatter.
I would love to paint you,
and you think you know what that means
beyond your own trivial daydreams.
You pretend
your beauty inspires,
that you are pretty enough,
mysterious enough,
permanent.

12.
The first time you missed him,
he stood next to you,
his attention focused on his own hands,
the charcoal,
the paper,
a cigarette dangling from his mouth.
He blinked around the smoke,
his motion blurred magic.

13.
You hold the rug between pinching fingers,
walk to the blue door peeling latex paint,
cradle crumbs and fingernail clippings
in the bowl of the shag carpet,
pieces of him caught in the nap,
throw open the screen against the wind,
shake it out, violent in the shimmer,
loosing your own tornado on the back porch.
He doesn't notice the missing rug when he returns home,
even though he's crossed it everyday of his life here,
the nap catching mud, grass from his shoes.
You want to point at the bare space,
fan your butterfly hands near his face,
but you are done with your graceless heart,
giving it all up to done.

14.
The first time you hated him,
he was smiling that white smile,
blazing,
but you couldn't laugh,
the sound choked off by stomach
because he didn't like you half as much
as you liked him,
Wasn't it all just the stupidest
thing you had ever done,
loving him,
alone.

15.
You are all mouth and tubular feet and hunger,
just tear-filled veins, a saltwater river covered with spines,
your phantom arms groping and starved.

Pregnant

1.
Counting down, day twenty-one, rolling around on the floor
in concentric, yogic patterns, all in a futile attempt to convince
baby to shift from right to left.

If gestation is any indication of future personality,
this child may be Nixon.
I lose my words somewhere between dinner and Wheel of Fortune.

2.
Day seventeen, baby is still rightly lodged,
back pressed firmly against ribs, so determined
to make her own room, flutter of feet visible
under the dome of my torso.

I've given up trying to look anything other than pregnant.
We watch my stomach more closely than television.

3.
Today I am a list, long and full of groceries
I will forget to put in meals.

I am a full balloon stuffed with flour and dried corn pellets.
A bladder.

4.
I am the drum, full round thrum of reverberations,
down through a future history not yet written,
a mother among a million other mothers,
waiting the last few moments before a new child enters the world,

A cliché in all its repetitions,
the rhythmic flare of a marching snare,
such a shattering new thing,
a quiet pebble dropped in still waters.

A Thousand Gallons of Water

I watch the water pour over her,
spitting out of the ground, a giant
cement lizard, hoping the
recycled and chlorinated dreams
of all those other children won't
taint or poison her. I feel shame
at my own shallow need that she
wear shoes. *She stubs her toes,*
I lie, even as I tell her one more
time to play with them on, as if
shoes can protect her from all the
sores and heartache. I wish I could
splash, be happy and naked and
shrug off a stubbed toe, be a
three-year-old with a Quik-Trip cup
and a thousand gallons of water.

Catfish

1.
Cool of chlorinated water slaps at our chins,
sun a baking heat drying out hair and face.

I clutch her four-year-old hand tightly,
only mildly reassured by her puddle jumper float
specifically designed to keep her head above water.

She's fearless, shockingly unafraid.
Powerful.
Fighting my grasping hand
like an unwilling catfish on my hook.

2.
I learned to swim when I was four,
tripping and falling into the deep-end
of our apartment complex swimming pool,

fell in, the water folding over my head,
sinking like a stone,
my mouth agape as I swallowed the chemical tang.

My feet touched bottom
       and I sprang,
              clawing my way to the top,

breaking surface enough to cough and scream
        and breathe
                and sink again,

my hands cupping palms of water,
moving me inexorably to shallow,

hopping like a hare chased by coyotes,
swimming my way to my aunt reclining supine in the sun,

where I promptly dumped her into the water
when I grabbed ahold of her float.

3.
I know I must let go. For my sake more than her,
that I must release the desperate cramp of my hand,
Blessed are they that come in the name of the lord,
but I know God doesn't protect us from pain,
that plenty of awful things happen to believers
and that God's 'plan' can be awful.

For a moment
I can't even pray
because what if it is God's will
and I'm having this crisis

all while my little catfish wants to swim away.

Eyes Closed

Shhhh he whispers against
the tender skin of your torso,
his breath moist,

his ideas similar to so many other ideas,
his hands warm against your nape,
small hairs caught for a moment

in the rough of his callus.
But your tired eyes see only a pile of dishes,
a swell of damp laundry,

the gas on E in your car
and the fatigue of the whole damn day
has you swallowing into sleep, today gone in the trees.

Before Dinner

Before dinner was left to congeal
in expensive copper bottom pot,
before we hid in porch shadow to watch
like it was primetime television,

before we spied on catty-corner neighbors
with the green Pontiac and broken muffler,
those same neighbors who gave out

Halloween peanut butter cups
instead of the Swedish Fish,
before those neighbors were screaming *fuck*
and *bastard* and *stupid cunt,*

before I held back your arm to keep
you from going down the driveway
because we were all clenched in fear
and excitement and wondering
if we should intervene, before all of that,

you curled your arms around me
while we stood in the kitchen,
hiding your nose in the crook of my neck,
in stillness for just a moment in rest, becalmed.

Skipping Stones

She casts her stone across
the still surface,
the splashing break of droplets
thrown forward
with force and momentum.
The whip-whine of sound—
dhew, d-dhew-dhew
like Atari's Centipede,
pant legs rolled to cuffs,
dirty knees,
bare feet in the shallow reed-bed,
squishing up soft mud through her toes.
Later, she'll learn
about the cells growing
in madness,
unstoppable,
even with nuclear war declared
on her body.
For now, she is a sweaty red handkerchief
and dirty feet
and a ripped tee-shirt hem.
She is the power in her arm,
the fluid, liquid motion of the casting hand,
the stone in flight, skipping over the water.

Fishes and Loaves

1.
Fishing for carp in enclosed docks
off of manmade lakes,
buildings floating in the gentle wake of boats.

Dropping corn or worms or freshly caught grasshopper
        jumbling around in whatever empty container
we could find,
a crest box minus the toothpaste tube,
only slightly wrinkled at the corner,
full of shoving, rattling hoppers,

Dropping them all down
into muddy water too sediment-filled to see,
water deep as death,
odor of scale and slime and fuel.

Who would eat from that filth?
But we would fish for the fun of the fight,
dragging innocent lives
onto the wooden planks of the piers.

2.
Worm Grunters earn their living scraping
an awl back and forth
across a wooden stake stabbed
into the heart of moist ground
of the Florida panhandle,
a place I have never been.

I should like to see them,
grunting and growling back and forth
As the worms crawl
out of the earth like searching fingers
to be gathered by the bucketful
only to die disastrously on the end of my hook.

3.
We didn't always throw them back.

She held in one hand a mallet.
The filleting knife, deceptively sharp,
Rests on the counter.
The other hand bare,
Her palm mashing into the eye above the gaping
        Swallowing
                Gasping
                        Mouth
I use it as a handle, she says,
remarking it's a reflex and I'm not to worry
because she won't slice until she's sure he's dead.

My eyes barely above the counter,
His ripe smell of lake and scale.

She brings the hammer over,
swinging to shatter what's left of his brains.

4.
I have admitted to No One
my extreme dislike of fishing

as it seems sacrileges:
Jesus was a fisher of men,

and while I, too, wish to net
 more souls for Jesus,
to see them pulled,
stunned from the water,

is too akin to my own stunned wakefulness.
I am always five, bending to the tug
and sway of the fishing line,
slicing ripples in the water, my brain frozen, gaping.

5.
Later, the sun will glare off the water,
My mother and I will slit our eyes in the orange.

I will step in her steps,
my shorter stride stretching out to match.
She will whistle a tuneless thread
And I will purse my lips, a fish gulping for air.

She will carry a can of Delmonte corn
and two fishing poles.
She is perfect then.

We will walk to a hidden pond
behind our apartment complex,
I will be lost in her shadow.

She will be teaching me to fish
before her next husband,
before our next move,
before the death of her father.

We will load our hooks with fat kernels
And drop them in the water.

We will smack at mosquitoes
and heat
and I will be perfect then, too.

Rain

1.
For fifty-six consecutive days,
nearly two months of nothing,
it did not rain.
Dark clouds occasionally threatened
from the far horizon,
lightning slamming to earth,
but they only choked on humidity
that wouldn't keep a promise.

2.
So it began with rain.
Or maybe it ended in the rain
as his car hydroplaned into the oncoming lane.
He would be sorry to know that he had done that,
caused that other family to have to buy a new car.

But now when it rained,
she can't drive her car,
can't breathe,
can't remember what it was like
to play in the downpour.

She can't see across the street
to the shallow metal mailbox,
where all his letters
used to land when he was away.

All the power of one stamp
affixed to the corner of his envelope,
wrinkling in wet transparency,
smearing blue ink to gray.

The rain comes down,
melting her hair into a sleek cap of gelatinous brown,
softening the skin of all her fingertips and toes.
The neighbors must think she's crazy.

3.
With rain comes wind,
flattening eyelids closed,
slamming against window shutters.
She leans,
embraces the fierce,
considers the flattening of her daffodils and marigolds.

She misses him.
The clutter of his keys and wallet
on the table by the door.

The stack of socks in shoes near his chair.
The bluster of his mad.

4.
She forces jackets on them,
though they complain,
warns them the wind is too high for umbrellas,

will just pop them inside out,
begs them not to jump in the puddles
get their socks all wet.

She hurts for a minute
because it would be easier if he were here,
but he's not and she's going to send them
out into the storm
to meet their bus for school.

The impulse to shelter them in the dry
has paralyzed her fingers in a c-shape
to keep herself from reaching for them, t
elling them to come back.

5.
They would watch the Weather Channel together.
He would tease that they weren't really old enough,

would marvel together
at the rainfall in some eastern town,

would pray their own drought broken,
hold hands as they sat together on the couch,
smiling at the antics and mess from the kids.

Someday she'll appreciate the wet again,
understand that it wasn't her fault,
that she wasn't even in the car,
that she'll quit tonguing the sore spot of his absence,
will hardly even notice his ghost anymore.

And the children will keep her busy,
will drag her into the rain.

April Pameticky moved to Wichita in 2003 and was swept up in the creative Vortex. The mother of two shares time between her high school English classroom and the burgeoning community of artists and writers in Kansas. She facilitated the Wichita Broadside Project 2017 and currently serves as editor of River City Poetry, an online poetry journal. Her own work can be seen in journals like *Malpais Review, KONZA,* and *Turtle Island Quarterly*. She is also the author of several chapbooks, *Sand River and Other Places I've Been* (2013, Finishing Line Press); and *Anatomy of a Sea Star* (2015, Casa de Cinco Hermanas Press).

This project was made possible, in part, by generous support from the Osage Arts Community.

Osage Arts Community provides temporary time, space and support for the creation of new artistic works in a retreat format, serving creative people of all kinds — visual artists, composers, poets, fiction and nonfiction writers. Located on a 152-acre farm in an isolated rural mountainside setting in Central Missouri and bordered by ¾ of a mile of the Gasconade River, OAC provides residencies to those working alone, as well as welcoming collaborative teams, offering living space and workspace in a country environment to emerging and mid-career artists. For more information, visit us at www.osageac.org

www.ingramcontent.com/pod-product-compliance
Lightning Source LLC
Chambersburg PA
CBHW030123100526
44591CB00009B/507